World Book's Human Body Works

The Endocrine System
The Reproductive System
Human Development

World Book, Inc.
a Scott Fetzer company
Chicago

World Book, Inc.
233 N. Michigan Ave.
Chicago, IL 60601 U.S.A.

For information about other World Book publications, visit our Web site at **http://www.worldbook.com** or call **1-800-WORLDBK (967-5325)**. For information about sales to schools and libraries, call **1-800-975-3250 (United States)**; **1-800-837-5365 (Canada)**.

World Book, Inc.
Editor in Chief: Paul A. Kobasa
Managing Editor: Maureen Mostyn Liebenson
Graphics and Design Manager: Sandra M. Dyrlund
Research Services Manager: Loranne K. Shields
Permissions Editor: Janet T. Peterson

Product development: Arcturus Publishing Limited
Writer: Carol Ballard
Editor: Alex Woolf
Designer: Jane Hawkins

Library of Congress Cataloging-in-Publication Data
The endocrine system, the reproductive system, human development.
    p. cm. -- (World Book's human body works)
    Summary: "An introduction to the endocrine and reproductive systems of the human body, and human development in general—one of six volumes in a set titled WORLD BOOK'S HUMAN BODY WORKS. Includes illustrations, glossary, resource list, and index"--Provided by publisher.
    Includes bibliographical references and index.
    ISBN-13: 978-0-7166-4431-6
    ISBN-10: 0-7166-4431-2
    1. Endocrine glands--Juvenile literature. 2. Generative organs--Juvenile literature. 3. Human reproduction--Juvenile literature.
I. World Book, Inc. II. Series.
QP187.E553 2007
612.4--dc22
                        2006013600
ISBN-13: 978-0-7166-4425-5 (set)
ISBN-10: 0-7166-4425-8 (set)

Printed in China

06 07 08 09 10 5 4 3 2 1

Acknowledgments
Corbis: cover and 35 (Jose Luis Pelaez, Inc.), 39 (Susan Johann), 43 (Leland Bobbé), 44 (Ole Graf, zefa), 45 (Cameron).
Michael Courtney: 6, 8, 10, 12, 14, 16, 17, 24, 26, 28, 42.
Science Photo Library: 4 (Bluestone), 5 (Scott Camazine), 7 (Alfred Pasieka), 9 (Michael Ross), 11 (Anatomical Travelogue), 13 (CNRI), 15 (Alfred Pasieka), 18 (John Bavosi), 19 (Professors P M Motta, K R Porter, and P M Andrews), 20 (Saturn Stills), 21 (John Paul Kay / Peter Arnold, Inc.), 22 (Brian Evans), 23 (Brian Evans), 25 (Bagavandoss), 27 (Dr Yorgos Nikas), 29 (Steve Gschmeissner), 30 (NIBSC), 31 (John Bavosi), 32 (D Phillips), 33 (Hank Morgan), 34 (Edelmann), 36 (John Greim), 37 (Larry Mulvehill), 38 (Andrew Syred), 40 (Tracy Dominey), 41 (BSIP, Chassenet).

Note: The content of this book does not constitute medical advice. Consult appropriate health-care professionals in matters of personal health, medical care, and fitness.

Features included in this book:

- **FAQs** Each spread contains an FAQ panel. FAQ stands for Frequently Asked Question. The panels contain answers to typical questions that relate to the topic of the spread.

- **Glossary** There is a glossary of terms on pages 46–47. Terms defined in the glossary are *italicized* on their first appearance on any spread.

- **Additional resources** Books for further reading and recommended Web sites are listed on page 47. Because of the nature of the Internet, some Web site addresses may have changed since publication. The publisher has no responsibility for any such changes nor for the content of cited resources.

Contents

The life cycle

All the stages in the life of a living thing make up its life cycle. Growth and reproduction are two basic life processes. Every type of living thing grows and reproduces at some stage during its life cycle. In this book you will find out about growth and reproduction in human beings and about the body systems that control these processes.

People's attitudes about some parts of the human life cycle, particularly those having to do with sexuality and reproduction, can be affected by customs and beliefs. These customs and beliefs can be based in traditions of a particular culture or teachings of a particular religion. People of good intention and character can disagree honestly over the acceptability of certain behaviors and practices. It is important to think about these issues with an open mind, respect others' points of view, and use accurate and reliable information in reaching conclusions about them.

Infancy and childhood

Think of some of the ways you have changed since you were born. You are bigger and stronger than you were as a newborn baby, and you have more hair on your head and a full set of teeth. You can control your muscles and

These females show different stages of the human life cycle.

movements and can talk and think. These changes happened during the first two stages of the human life cycle: infancy and childhood. Infancy is the period from birth until about the age of 18 months. Childhood extends from 18 months to about 10 to 12 years of age.

Adolescence, adulthood, and old age

The third stage in the human life cycle is adolescence. During adolescence the final growing phase occurs, along with other physical and mental developments that accompany the change from childhood to adulthood. In healthy people, adolescence usually begins between the ages of 10 and 12.

Adulthood follows adolescence. It is the longest stage of the human life cycle. Most healthy adults stop growing and developing between the ages of 18 and 30. Their weight may continue to increase, however. Although reproduction becomes possible during adolescence, it more commonly takes place during adulthood.

The final stage of the human life cycle is old age. When old age occurs varies greatly, but by the time people reach their mid-60s, their muscles and bones often become weaker. Other changes occur, too, such as loss of hearing and graying hair.

What controls the life cycle?

The endocrine system controls the human life cycle. The endocrine system is a complex network of body structures and the substances they produce. The endocrine system is made up of *glands* that produce chemicals called *hormones*. The hormones circulate in the blood, affecting different parts and functions of the body. Hormones are often called "chemical messengers." Although hormones' effects may not always be noticed immediately, most are long lasting.

The life cycle of an insect, such as this butterfly, is different from the human life cycle.

FAQ

Q. What controls human growth?

A. One of the hormones produced by the endocrine system is called growth hormone, or GH. Among other effects, GH makes bones grow longer and increases the size and strength of muscles. The amount of GH produced by the endocrine system determines how much we will grow. Lots of GH means lots of growth; little GH means little growth. GH is produced mainly during infancy, childhood, and adolescence.

The endocrine system

The endocrine system produces chemicals called *hormones* that regulate (control) much of what happens inside the human body.

Function

The *glands* and hormones of the endocrine system play a vital part in maintaining a healthy and active body. Such functions as sleep, digestion, *urine* production, blood pressure, heartbeat, and breathing rate are regulated by hormones. Without hormones, growth and development would not take place and reproduction would be impossible.

The main functions of the endocrine system are:
- regulation of growth and development
- regulation of chemical reactions and body processes
- preparation of the body to react to danger or stress.

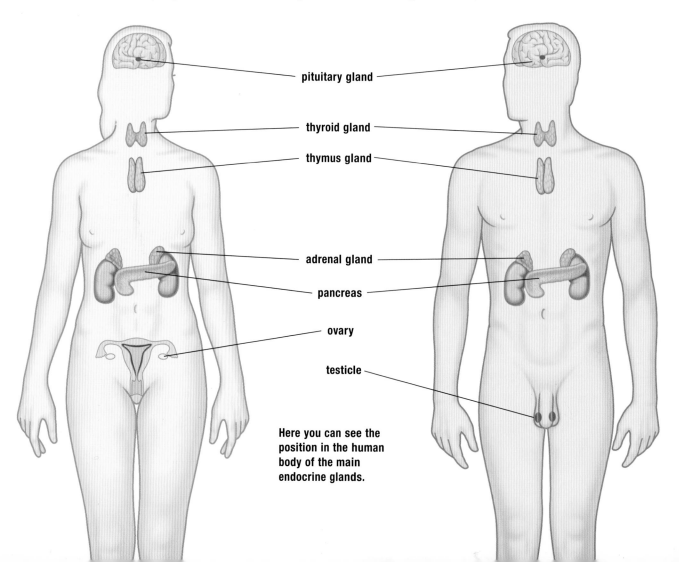

pituitary gland

thyroid gland

thymus gland

adrenal gland

pancreas

ovary

testicle

Here you can see the position in the human body of the main endocrine glands.

Glands

A gland is a collection of *cells* that work together to produce and release chemicals. Endocrine glands produce hormones. Endocrine glands do not have ducts (tubes) to carry the hormones away. Instead, the hormones pass straight from the glands into the bloodstream and are carried throughout the body. The main endocrine glands are found in the head, neck, chest, and abdomen.

How hormones work

Hormones themselves do not carry out body processes, but they make other parts of the body respond and react in particular ways. Hormones are not produced all the time— the glands produce them only when a particular job needs to be done.

There are two types of hormones: those that are made of up *protein* and those that are not. Most of the hormones are of the first type. The nonprotein hormones, called steroids, include the sex hormones. Both types of hormones travel in the blood. When they reach their target—that is, the organ or *tissue* they affect— they combine with special cells called receptors. Protein hormones attach themselves to the surface of the receptors. Steroids penetrate (move through) the outer layer of the receptors and get right inside.

This model shows the complex structure of a hormone molecule.

FAQ

Q. What are exocrine glands?

A. Exocrine glands are glands that have ducts that carry a substance away from the gland where it was made. Exocrine glands produce substances that perform various functions. Sweat glands in the skin, which produce sweat, are exocrine glands. The evaporation of sweat from the skin's surface helps cool the body. Salivary glands in the mouth, which produce saliva, are also exocrine glands. Saliva is important in the digestion of food. Exocrine glands are not part of the endocrine system.

Pituitary gland, hypothalamus, and pineal gland

The *pituitary gland*, *hypothalamus*, and *pineal gland* are all parts of the endocrine system that are found in or close to the brain.

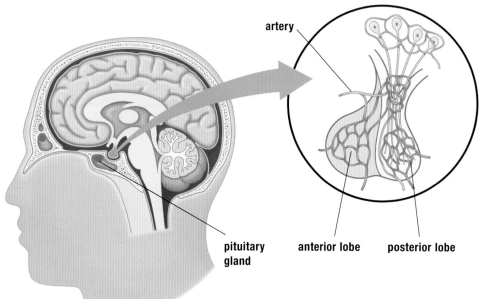

artery

pituitary gland

anterior lobe

posterior lobe

This diagram shows the pituitary gland lying deep in the brain. Inset: a magnified view of the pituitary gland.

Pituitary gland

The pituitary gland sits in a protective, cup-shaped dip in one of the skull bones. It has two lobes, or parts. The anterior, or front, lobe produces and releases *hormones*, and the posterior, or back, lobe is supplied with hormones directly from the hypothalamus, which the posterior lobe then releases.

The pituitary gland itself is controlled by the hypothalamus. Although the pituitary gland is only about the size of a pea, the hormones it releases control many of the other endocrine glands. This table shows some of the hormones released by the pituitary gland, the hormones' target organs, and the hormones' effects.

Hormones produced and released by the anterior lobe

Hormone	Target organs	Effects
growth hormone (GH)	bones and muscles	regulates growth
prolactin	mammary glands in breasts	stimulates mother's milk production after birth of her baby
follicle-stimulating hormone (FSH) and luteinizing hormone (LH)	sex glands	reproductive functions
thyroid-stimulating hormone (TSH)	thyroid	stimulates production of thyroid hormones
adrenocorticotropic hormone (ACTH)	adrenal glands	stimulates production of adrenal hormones
endorphins	central nervous system	help the body respond to pain or stress

Hypothalamus

The hypothalamus is an important control center that regulates the pituitary gland and also parts of the nervous system. The hypothalamus receives information directly from other parts of the brain and from sense organs in other parts of the body. The hypothalamus uses the information it receives to help control such functions as body temperature, hunger, thirst, heart rate, and sleep, as well as some emotions, such as anger and fear.

A variety of different hormones is produced and released by the hypothalamus. Some pass straight to the posterior lobe of the pituitary gland and from it to the rest of the body. Others travel in the bloodstream to the anterior lobe of the pituitary gland, where they stimulate the production and release of pituitary gland hormones.

Hormones produced by the hypothalamus and released by the posterior lobe

Hormone	Target organs	Effects
antidiuretic hormone (ADH)	kidneys	maintains water level in blood
oxytocin	uterus and mammary glands	contractions during childbirth; release of milk

FAQ

Q. What is the "master gland"?

A. In the past, some people called the pituitary gland the master gland. This was because the pituitary controls other glands. But scientists now know that the pituitary gland has a controller of its own: the hypothalamus. So maybe the hypothalamus really should be called the master gland!

Pineal gland

The pineal gland is a tiny gland deep in the center of the brain. Although scientists are not certain about the pineal gland's function, they know this gland receives information from the eyes and produces and releases a hormone called melatonin. Scientists think that melatonin may play a part in the "jet lag" that many people experience when they travel in an airplane across several time zones. Melatonin also may play a part in causing some forms of mental illness, and it may be linked to sexual development.

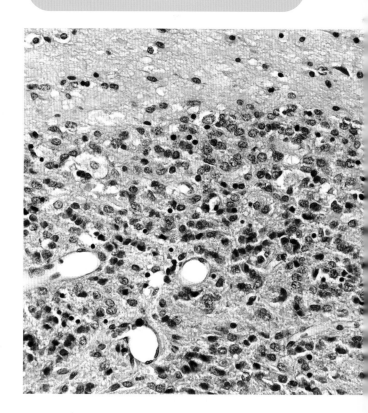

This micrograph (a photograph taken through a microscope) shows the cells of the pineal gland.

Thyroid and parathyroid glands

The *thyroid gland* and the *parathyroid glands* are found in the neck. The thyroid gland lies around the front and sides of the windpipe. The parathyroid glands are buried in the back of the thyroid gland.

Thyroid gland

The thyroid has two lobes, or parts, one on each side of the windpipe. They are linked by a band of *tissue* called the isthmus. The thyroid gland is made up of hundreds of thousands of small chambers. These chambers produce the thyroid *hormones* and store them until they are needed.

The thyroid makes, stores, and releases several different hormones. One of the most important is thyroxine. It affects our growth rate, mental activity, body temperature, and general energy levels. Another important thyroid hormone is calcitonin, which helps control the amount of the mineral calcium in the blood.

This diagram shows the position of the thyroid gland. Inset: a detail of the thyroid gland's internal structure.

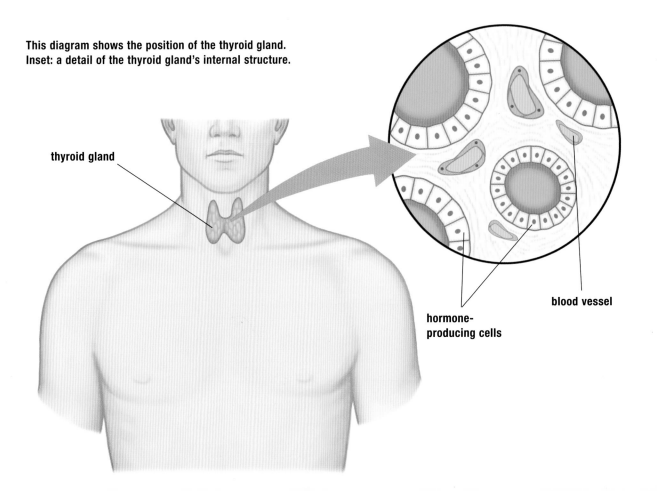

thyroid gland

blood vessel

hormone-producing cells

Parathyroid glands

Each parathyroid gland is about 0.5 inch (13 millimeters) in diameter. There are usually four of them, two in each lobe of the thyroid. Although parathyroid glands are very small, they are important. They produce a hormone called parathyroid hormone, or PTH. This helps control the levels of two minerals—calcium and phosphate—in the blood. The minerals are important for bone growth and muscle and nerve function.

Controlling calcium in the blood

Together, calcitonin and PTH regulate the amount of calcium in the blood. They have opposite effects. If the calcium level gets too low, PTH is released. The release of PTH increases the calcium level by unlocking calcium stored in the bones, by making the digestive system absorb more calcium from food, and by preventing the kidneys from getting rid of calcium in the *urine*.

If the calcium level gets too high, the PTH release stops and calcitonin is released instead. The release of calcitonin reduces the calcium level by making the kidneys get rid of more calcium in the urine and by making the bones store more calcium. Together, these two hormones maintain the amount of calcium in the blood at the right level.

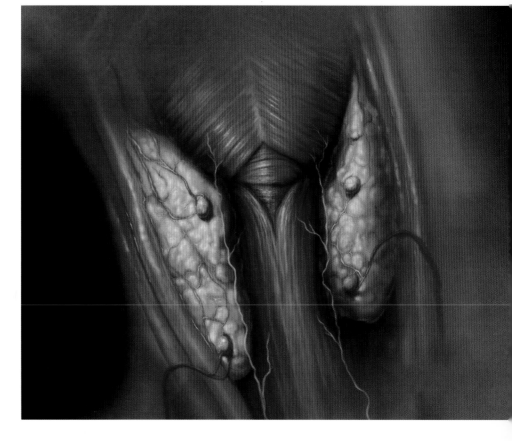

An illustration of the thyroid and parathyroid glands. The parathyroid glands are the small, pea-shaped structures.

FAQ

Q. How can thyroid hormones help warm and cool the body?

A. Thyroid hormones regulate the chemical reactions in the body's cells. These reactions, together known as metabolism, make the energy the body needs. High levels of thyroxine speed up metabolism. A fast metabolism produces more heat, so the body stays warm. Lower levels of thyroxine slow down metabolism. Less heat is produced, and the body cools. Changes in the level of thyroxine are part of a healthy body's self-regulation system.

Thymus gland

The *thymus* is a *gland* that lies in the chest, behind the breastbone and just above the heart. The thymus has two lobes, or parts, which are held together by connective *tissue*. Each lobe itself has two parts: the cortex, which is the outer part, and the medulla, in the center.

Defending the body

Scientists are unsure if the thymus gland should or should not be thought of as part of the endocrine system. This is because a major part of the thymus gland's job has little to do with *hormones*. The thymus turns white blood *cells* known as lymphocytes into T cells, which help defend the body against germs and diseases. (The "T" stands for thymus derived, because these cells come from the thymus.) Because of this, for many years scientists simply regarded the thymus as part of the body's immune, or defense, system.

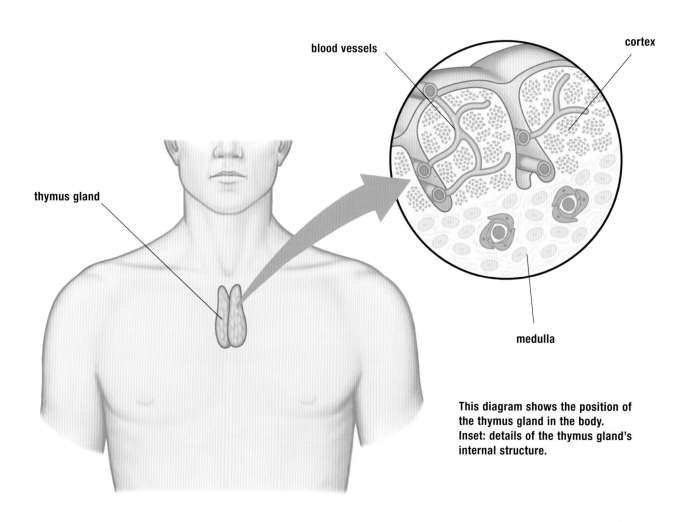

blood vessels

cortex

thymus gland

medulla

This diagram shows the position of the thymus gland in the body. Inset: details of the thymus gland's internal structure.

Producing hormones

However, the thymus also produces hormones, and so it is an endocrine gland as well. The hormones produced by the thymus are thymosin, thymic humoral factor, thymulin, and thymopoietin. They help T cells to mature and develop. They also help some other white blood cells, called B cells, to develop.

Scientists believe that the thymus might have another job, too. Recent studies have shown that the thymus may play a part in controlling hormone production by the *pituitary gland*.

Living without a thymus

Although the thymus is important, people can live without it. Some babies are born without a thymus. They grow and develop normally in most ways, but their immune systems do not function properly. To treat some illnesses in adults, surgeons may remove the thymus. This does not seem to affect the adult immune system at all.

FAQ

Q. How big is the thymus?

A. The size of the thymus varies with a person's age. A newborn's thymus usually weighs about 0.4 to 0.5 ounce (11 to 15 grams). It continues to grow until the early teenage years, when the thymus is at its biggest and most active. Then it weighs about 1 ounce (30 grams). After that, it begins to shrink and slowly becomes less active because other parts of the body take over making lymphocytes and the thymus makes fewer T cells.

A micrograph showing lymphocytes inside the cortex of the thymus.

Adrenal glands

The human body has two *adrenal glands*, one on top of each kidney. Each adrenal gland is a squashed pyramid shape. In an adult, an adrenal gland is about 2 inches (5 centimeters) high, about 0.8 to 1.2 inch (2 to 3 centimeters) wide, and about 0.4 inch (1 centimeter) thick.

Each adrenal gland is made up of two parts: an outer part called the cortex and an inner part called the medulla. These two parts are surrounded by an outer covering called the capsule. The *hormones* produced and released by the cortex and medulla have very different effects.

Cortex

The cortex produces hormones called corticosteroids. These hormones help control the way the body uses such substances as sugars and starches, *proteins*, and fats. Corticosteroids also control the level of water and some minerals in the blood. Corticosteroids affect the sex organs and growth and development during puberty (see pages 42–43). These hormones also play a part in controlling some allergic reactions and in helping the body adapt to stress.

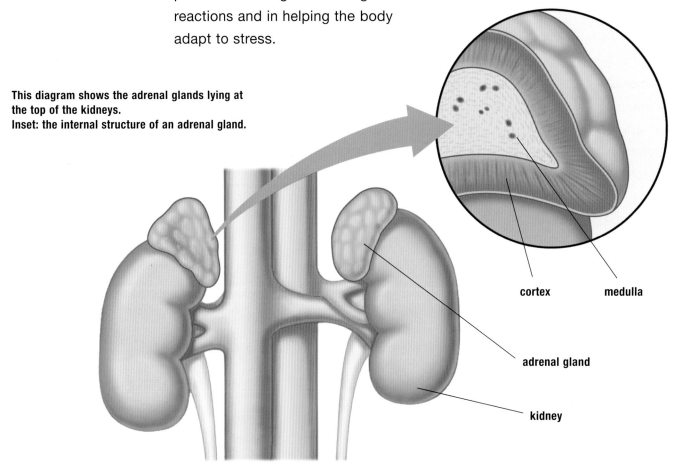

This diagram shows the adrenal glands lying at the top of the kidneys.
Inset: the internal structure of an adrenal gland.

cortex   medulla

adrenal gland

kidney

FAQ

Q. Why does the body produce epinephrine and norepinephrine?

A. In other animals, the effects of these hormones prepare the animal to defend itself or run from danger. Today, people do not usually need to react to danger in this way, but our bodies get ready just in case!

This photograph shows crystals of epinephrine, magnified about 50 times.

Medulla

The medulla produces one main hormone called epinephrine (also called adrenalin). The medulla is linked directly to the brain by nerves. When you are frightened or anxious, signals from the brain stimulate the adrenal glands to produce and release two hormones, epinephrine and norepinephrine. These hormones travel rapidly in the blood throughout the body. Their effects, which are seen and felt almost immediately, include the following:

- increased heart rate and blood pressure
- increased breathing rate
- skin turns pale
- stomach feels hollow and "fluttery"
- muscles tense.

When your brain decides that you are safe, it sends a signal to the adrenal medulla. This stops the production of epinephrine, and your body systems slowly return to normal.

Ovaries and testicles

The *ovaries* are female sex organs, and the *testicles* are male sex organs. Both produce sex *hormones* that affect the reproductive system. The sex hormones also play an important part in the changes that occur during puberty (see pages 42–43).

Ovaries and their hormones

A woman has two ovaries, one on each side of the uterus in the lower *abdomen*. Each ovary is a small organ about the same size and shape as an unshelled walnut. An ovary is made up of two areas: an outer layer called the cortex, which is full of hundreds of thousands of unripe egg *cells*, and a central part, the medulla, which contains blood vessels.

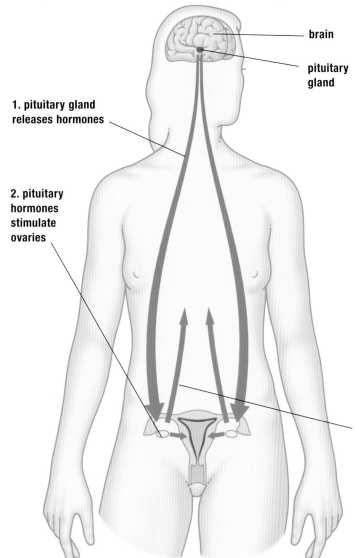

brain

pituitary gland

1. pituitary gland releases hormones

2. pituitary hormones stimulate ovaries

3. ovaries release estrogen and progesterone

The ovaries produce the hormones estrogen and progesterone. Together with hormones from the *pituitary gland*, estrogen and progesterone control the ripening of egg cells and the female reproductive cycle. These hormones are the main causes of the changes that occur in girls' bodies at puberty, such as widening of the hips. Estrogen and progesterone also are important during pregnancy.

Ovaries produce two more hormones called relaxin and inhibin. Relaxin widens the birth canal during birth. Inhibin affects the production of some pituitary hormones.

This diagram shows how the release of hormones from the pituitary gland affects the rest of the female body.

Testicles and their hormones

The testicles, also called testes, are egg-shaped organs about 1.5 inches (4 centimeters) long and 1.25 inches (3 centimeters) wide in adult men that lie outside the abdomen in a protective sack of skin called the *scrotum*. Each testicle contains hundreds of tightly coiled tubes, which produce *sperm* cells. Between these tubes are areas where sex hormones, called androgens, are produced.

The most important male sex hormone is testosterone. Hormones from the pituitary gland control its production. Testosterone is the main cause of the changes that occur in boys' bodies at puberty, such as sperm production. It also affects other male characteristics, such as beard growth and the deepening of the voice.

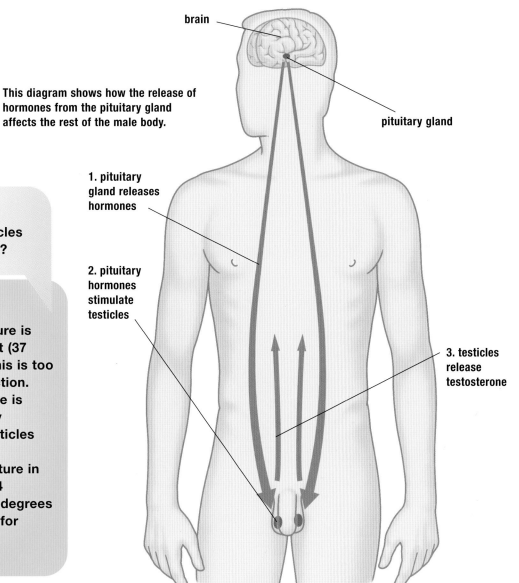

This diagram shows how the release of hormones from the pituitary gland affects the rest of the male body.

brain

pituitary gland

1. pituitary gland releases hormones

2. pituitary hormones stimulate testicles

3. testicles release testosterone

FAQ

Q. Why are the testicles outside the abdomen?

A. A healthy person's internal body temperature is 98.6 degrees Fahrenheit (37 degrees Celsius), but this is too warm for sperm production. The outside temperature is usually lower than body temperature, so the testicles are cooler outside the abdomen. The temperature in the testicles is about 94 degrees Fahrenheit (34 degrees Celsius), which is ideal for sperm production.

Other endocrine glands

Endocrine glands are also found in other parts of the body, including the *pancreas*, stomach, heart, and kidneys.

The pancreas

The pancreas lies in the upper *abdomen*, in front of the kidneys and mainly behind the liver and stomach. It is usually about 6 to 8 inches (15 to 20 centimeters) long. It works as both an *exocrine gland* and an endocrine gland. Most of its *cells* produce chemicals involved in digestion. This is the pancreas's exocrine function. Other cells in the pancreas produce *hormones*. This is the pancreas's endocrine function.

The pancreas produces four hormones:

- insulin
- glucagon
- somatostatin
- pancreatic polypeptide.

Insulin and glucagon

Insulin and glucagon work together to control the amount of glucose in the blood. Glucose is a form of sugar and is the main fuel of the body's cells. The amount of glucose in the blood must be kept at a steady level for good health. If the glucose level gets too high, the pancreas releases insulin. This reduces the glucose level

**This diagram shows the position of the pancreas below the liver.
Inset: a detail of the internal structure of the pancreas.**

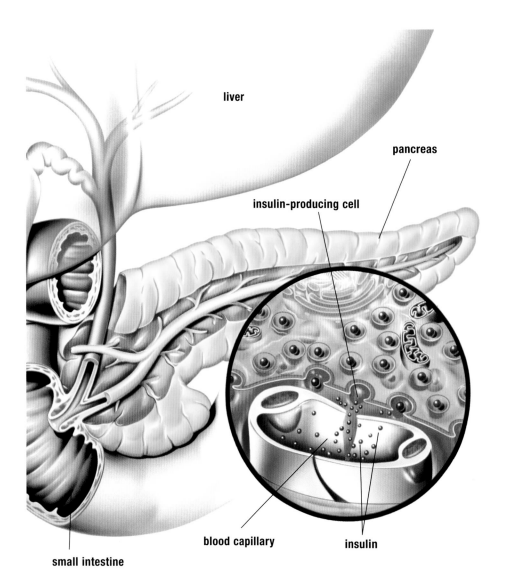

liver

pancreas

insulin-producing cell

blood capillary

insulin

small intestine

by making the liver take glucose out of the blood and store it. If the glucose level gets too low, the pancreas stops releasing insulin and releases glucagon instead. This raises the glucose level in the blood by making the liver release some of its stored glucose. Together, these two hormones maintain the amount of glucose in the blood at the right level.

Somatostatin and pancreatic polypeptide

Somatostatin helps control the production of insulin and glucagon. Pancreatic polypeptide helps control several processes in the body, including the release of digestive chemicals by the pancreas.

FAQ

Q. Which hormones are produced in other parts of the body?

A. Some of the hormones produced in other parts of the body include:

- Atrial natriuretic peptide, produced by the heart, works with the kidneys to help lower blood pressure
- Erythropoietin, produced by the kidneys, increases production of red blood cells
- Leptin, produced by fatty tissue, affects hunger
- Gastrin, produced by the stomach, causes production of digestive juices
- Secretin, produced by the small intestine, stimulates production of digestive juices in the pancreas.

A magnified view of the entrance to a gland in the lining of the stomach.

Disorders of the endocrine system

The endocrine system is complex, involving many *glands* and *hormones*, so it is not surprising that it does not always work properly. Problems associated with the endocrine system include diabetes and disorders of the *pituitary* and *thyroid glands*.

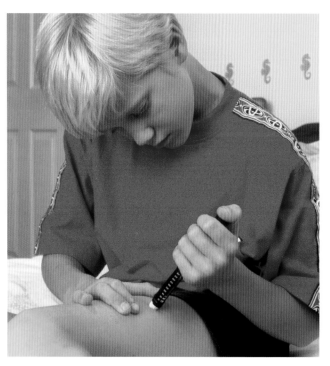

This boy is diabetic and needs to inject insulin into his body regularly.

FAQ

Q. How common is diabetes?

A. In the United States, nearly 15 million people know they have diabetes. Most of these people have Type 2 diabetes. However, doctors think that the total number of people with diabetes is really much higher because many people have diabetes without realizing it.

Diabetes

Diabetes is one of the most common endocrine disorders. People who suffer from diabetes are said to be diabetic. Their bodies do not produce and use insulin properly, and they are unable to control the amount of sugar in their blood. The two types of diabetes are called Type 1 and Type 2.

Type 1 diabetes usually affects younger people. The *pancreas* does not produce enough insulin, so the blood sugar level rises. A person with Type 1 diabetes often requires daily injections of insulin.

Type 2 diabetes usually affects middle-aged and older people, especially if they are overweight. The pancreas produces normal amounts of insulin, but the body does not respond properly to it. Type 2 diabetes can often be controlled by changes in the diet.

Pituitary gland problems

The pituitary gland produces growth hormone (GH), which controls how much a person's body grows. Too much GH causes a person to grow more than normal. This is called giantism. People suffering from giantism may grow to 9 feet (274 centimeters) tall.

Too little GH means a person does not grow as much as normal. This is called pituitary dwarfism. A person with this condition may have the body shape of an adult but be the same height as a six-year-old child.

Thyroid gland problems

In some people the thyroid gland may be overactive, whereas in others it may be underactive. An overactive thyroid produces too much thyroxine. People with overactive thyroids are generally nervous, irritable, and unable to sleep, and have a fast heart rate, diarrhea, and bulging eyes. An overactive thyroid can be treated with drugs to reduce the amount of thyroxine produced, or by removing part of the thyroid.

An underactive thyroid produces too little thyroxine. This condition may be inherited or caused by a lack of iodine in the diet. An underactive thyroid in adults causes tiredness, dry skin, a slow heart rate, and poor memory. It can also lead to a swelling in the neck called a goiter. If the thyroid is underactive during the early weeks of an *embryo's* development, brain development and bone and muscle growth can be affected. The condition can be treated with thyroxine.

This boy's growth and development have been affected by a thyroid disorder.

The reproductive system

The reproductive system in human beings is made up of the organs that enable a woman and a man together to begin a pregnancy (create a baby). The reproductive system of a woman is different from that of a man. *Cells* from each system must be combined to create a baby.

The female reproductive organs

The organs that make up the female reproductive system are in the lower *abdomen*. Most of the organs are inside a woman's body, where they are supported and protected by a strong ring of bones called the pelvic girdle. These organs include those that produce egg cells from which a baby may develop. They also include the uterus, which is the organ that provides an environment in which the unborn baby can grow and develop in the months before it is born. This period is known as pregnancy.

This diagram shows a side view through the center of the female reproductive organs.

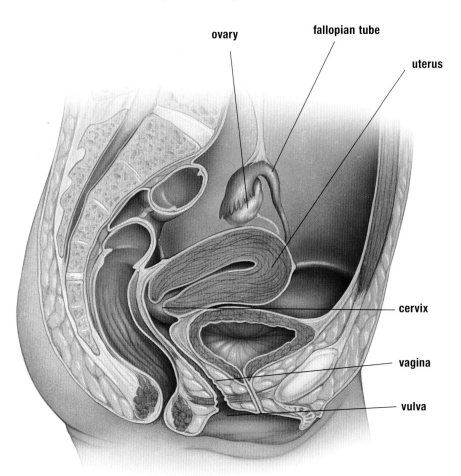

ovary

fallopian tube

uterus

cervix

vagina

vulva

The main organs of the female reproductive system are:

- *ovaries*, two organs that produce, store, and release eggs and produce *hormones*
- *fallopian tubes*, which link the ovaries and uterus
- *uterus*, the hollow, muscular organ in which an unborn baby grows and develops until birth
- *cervix*, the opening between the uterus and the vagina
- *vagina*, the canal that links the uterus and the outside of the body
- *vulva*, the sex organs, outside the lower abdomen, between the legs, which help protect the inner organs.

(See also pages 24–25).

The male reproductive organs

The organs of the male reproductive system are also in the lower abdomen. Some lie inside the abdomen, and others are outside it. Two of these organs produce *sperm* cells, which can join with egg cells from a woman to conceive, or begin the creation of, a baby. The male reproductive system includes the *penis*, which is the organ that deposits, or places, the sperm in a woman's body.

The main organs of the male reproductive system are:
- *testicles*, two organs that produce sperm cells; the testicles are suspended outside the lower abdomen in a small sack of skin called the *scrotum*, between the legs and behind the penis
- *epididymis* and *vas deferens*, ducts (tubes) through which sperm cells travel from the testicles to the *prostate gland*
- prostate gland and seminal vesicles, together known as the accessory glands, which provide fluids to lubricate the ducts and feed the sperm; sperm cells are mixed into the fluid to make *semen*
- penis, a cylindrical organ outside the lower abdomen, in front of the scrotum, between the legs, containing the urethra, the tube through which semen and urine pass out of the body.

(See also pages 28–29.)

FAQ

Q. What is circumcision?

A. Circumcision is the cutting away of the foreskin, the fold of skin that covers the tip of the penis. Circumcision usually is done when a baby boy is a few days old. It may be done for religious or cultural reasons. It also may be done for health reasons, because research shows that circumcision can reduce the risk of infections.

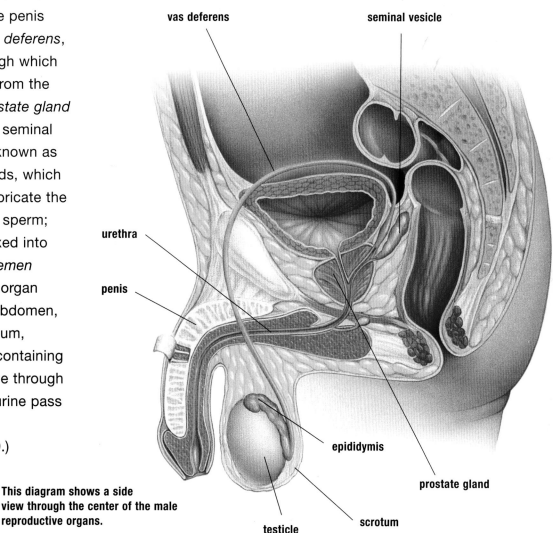

vas deferens — seminal vesicle — urethra — penis — epididymis — prostate gland — testicle — scrotum

This diagram shows a side view through the center of the male reproductive organs.

Female reproductive system

The organs of the human female reproductive system include those that supply egg *cells* that can combine with cells from the male reproductive system to create babies. One of these organs provides an environment in which an unborn baby can grow and develop in the months before birth. The main parts of the female reproductive system are the *ovaries*, *fallopian tubes*, *uterus*, *cervix*, *vagina*, and *vulva*.

The organs of the female reproductive system.

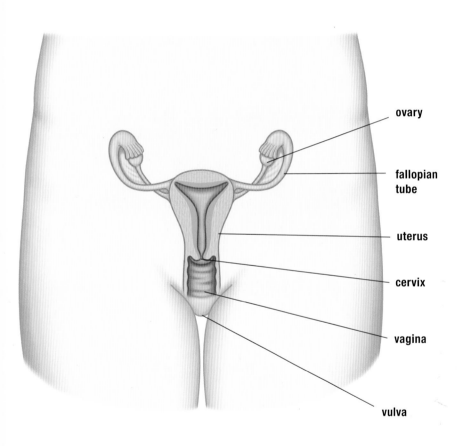

ovary

fallopian tube

uterus

cervix

vagina

vulva

Ovaries, fallopian tubes, and uterus

When a girl is born, her two ovaries already contain hundreds of thousands of egg cells. When she reaches puberty, the ovaries begin to release *hormones* that allow one egg cell to ripen each month. When the egg cell is ripe, it leaves the ovary.

The two fallopian tubes are hollow, muscular canals. Each forms a link between one ovary and the uterus. The fallopian tubes are often called oviducts. In adult women, each is about 4 inches (10 centimeters) long and is about as thick as a pencil. Ripe egg cells travel through the fallopian tubes to the uterus.

The uterus is the place where an unborn baby grows. The uterus has thick walls made of strong expandable muscle. In an adult woman who is not pregnant, the uterus is shaped like an upside-down pear and is about the size of a fist. The uterus expands about 24 times its usual size during pregnancy. The inner lining of the uterus, called the endometrium, contains many blood vessels.

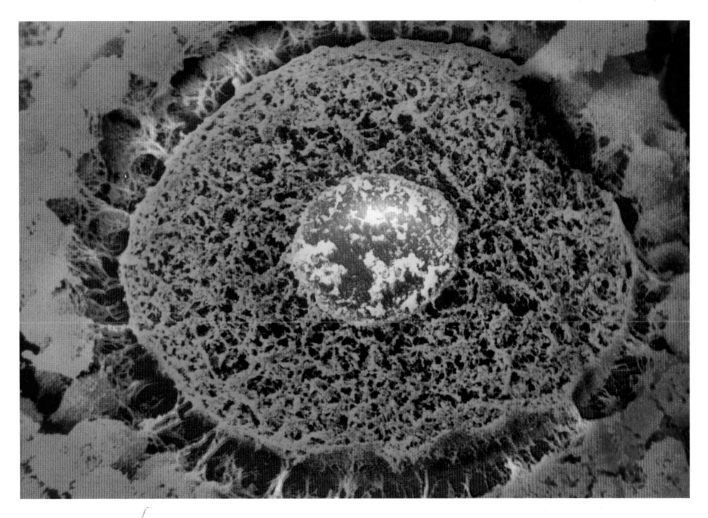

Cervix, vagina, and vulva

The cervix is the narrow lower end of the uterus. It is a hollow tube, linking the uterus and vagina. The vagina is a muscular tube about 4 inches (10 centimeters) long.

The vulva is the name for the female sex organs that lie outside the body at the base of the *abdomen*, between the legs. The vulva includes the outer and inner labia, the clitoris, and the mons. The outer and inner labia are folds of skin and fatty tissue that help to protect the vaginal opening. The labia also cover the opening of the *urethra*, through which *urine* leaves the body. The clitoris is a tiny organ about the size of a pea, which is very sensitive. The mons is a fatty mound in front of the pubic bone that is covered by pubic hair in adults.

A highly magnified photograph of a human egg cell.

FAQ

Q. What is an egg cell like?

A. An egg cell resembles a ball about 0.004 inch (0.1 millimeter) across. In the middle is the nucleus, which contains all the genetic information. The nucleus is surrounded by a nourishing substance. A thin outer layer holds the nucleus together. This is surrounded by a thick, jellylike coat.

The menstrual cycle

The menstrual cycle is a pattern of events, controlled by *hormones*, that takes place roughly once every month in the *ovaries* and *uterus* of a woman's body. This process prepares a woman to become pregnant. Most healthy girls experience their first menstrual cycle between the ages of 10 and 16.

The stages of the menstrual cycle

About once a month, a few eggs begin to mature in the ovaries. At the same time, the ovary releases the hormone estrogen. This makes the uterus begin to prepare for a baby. The uterus lining, the endometrium, thickens and softens in preparation for protecting and nurturing the new life. After about 14 days, one of the eggs becomes fully mature, and it is released from the ovary. This is called *ovulation*.

After ovulation, the ovary switches from releasing estrogen to releasing progesterone instead. The mature egg enters the *fallopian tube* and travels slowly toward the uterus. Tiny hairs called cilia on the inside of the fallopian tube help move the egg along. Once the egg leaves the ovary, it has a short life span. Unless an egg unites with a *sperm cell* and becomes fertilized, it can survive for only about 24 hours in the fallopian tube.

If the egg does not become fertilized, the uterus lining breaks down and leaves the body through the *vagina*. This loss of lining and blood is called *menstruation*, or having a period. Menstruation occurs about 14 days after ovulation. The cycle then begins all over again as the ovary switches back to releasing estrogen and a new egg ripens.

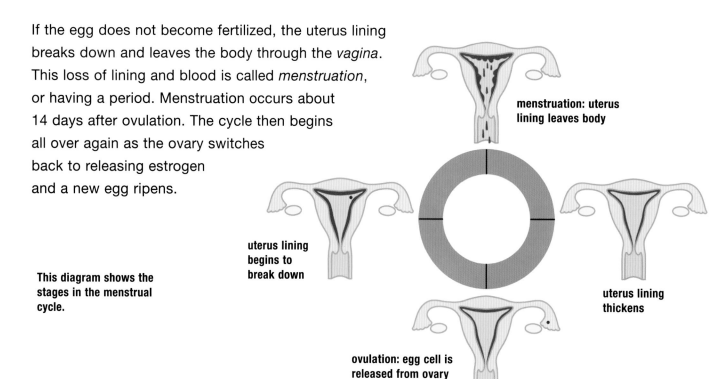

This diagram shows the stages in the menstrual cycle.

menstruation: uterus lining leaves body

uterus lining begins to break down

uterus lining thickens

ovulation: egg cell is released from ovary

A magnified cross-section of the thickened uterus lining at the time of ovulation.

Frequency and length of the menstrual cycle

Most women have a period about once a month. Each period lasts from three to seven days. In many women, however, the time between periods may be longer or shorter. Periods may be irregular, especially during adolescence, when the body's natural cycle is still developing.

Menopause

The menstrual cycle does not continue throughout a woman's life. By the age of about 50 in most women, the cycle becomes irregular and eventually stops altogether. When the cycle stops, eggs stop ripening, and sex hormones are not produced. This stopping of the menstrual cycle is called menopause.

FAQ

Q. What is PMS?

A. Pre-menstrual syndrome, or PMS, is the name given to the way many women feel in the days before their period begins. PMS is probably caused by the hormonal changes that take place during this part of the menstrual cycle. Symptoms of PMS include headaches, irritability, tiredness, sore breasts, and discomfort in the lower *abdomen*.

Male reproductive system

The organs of the human male reproductive system include those that produce the *sperm cells* that can combine with cells in the female reproductive system to create babies. The system includes an organ for depositing the sperm cells inside a woman's body. The main parts of the male reproductive system are the *testicles*, *epididymides*, *vas deferentia*, *prostate gland*, seminal vesicles, *urethra*, and *penis*.

Testicles, epididymis, and vas deferens

The two testicles are the organs that produce sperm cells. They lie outside the body in a loose sack of skin called the *scrotum*, at the base of the abdomen, between the legs and behind the penis. Inside each testicle is a complex network of tiny tubes. Sperm are produced inside these tubes. When they are nearly mature, the sperm move out into the epididymides.

The epididymis is a long, coiled tube that lies over the back of each testicle. Sperm reach full maturity inside the epididymis after about 12 days. The mature sperm then are stored in the epididymis.

The vas deferentia are two tubes that form a link between the epididymis of each testicle and the urethra. They are often called sperm ducts. When sperm leave the epididymides, they travel through the vas deferentia toward the urethra.

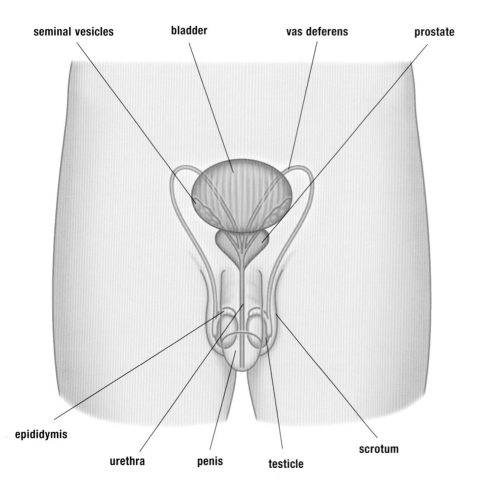

seminal vesicles   bladder   vas deferens   prostate

epididymis   urethra   penis   testicle   scrotum

The organs of the male reproductive system.

Seminal vesicles, urethra, and penis

The seminal vesicles, together with the *prostate gland*, produce a liquid called seminal fluid. This mixes with the sperm. Together, the seminal fluid and sperm are called *semen*.

The urethra is a tube that runs from the urinary bladder to the tip of the penis. The vas deferentia are also linked to it. The urethra has two jobs: carrying *urine* and semen to the outside of the body. Only one fluid is carried at any one time.

Most of the time, the penis hangs limp. Inside the penis are special *tissues* that can fill with blood. When this happens, the penis becomes stiff and hard. This is called an erection, and it usually happens when a man is sexually excited. Abdominal muscles contract when the erect penis is stimulated, and seminal fluid is forced out of the penis. This is called ejaculation.

Sperm cells, magnified around 2,500 times.

FAQ

Q. What is a sperm cell like?

A. A sperm cell is similar to a tadpole in shape, with an oval head and a long thin tail. It is tiny—just over 0.00012 inch (0.003 millimeter) across and 0.002 inch (0.05 millimeter) long. In the head of the sperm is the nucleus, which contains all the genetic information. Around the nucleus is a small amount of nutritious material. The head is held together by a thin outer layer. At the end of the head is a tail, which helps the sperm to swim.

Disorders of the reproductive system

Disorders of the reproductive system may affect a person's own health or his or her ability to conceive a baby. Some disorders arise within the person's own body, whereas others may be passed from one person to another.

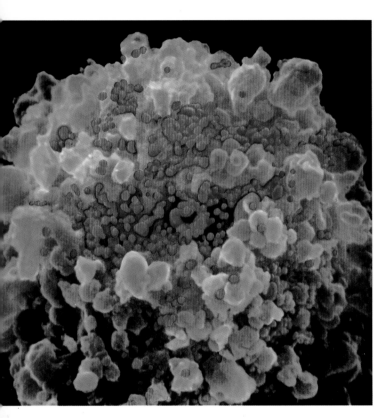

This lymphocyte (green) has been infected by the HIV virus (red).

Sexually transmitted diseases (STDs)

Sexually transmitted diseases, or STDs, pass from one person to another through sexual and other contact in which body fluids are exchanged. STDs are infections caused by such microbes as bacteria and viruses. Some of the most common STDs include chlamydia, gonorrhea, syphilis, and human immunodeficiency virus (HIV). STDs can permanently damage the reproductive organs. These diseases can affect a person's ability to have children and can harm an unborn baby. Syphilis, if untreated, can damage the brain and nervous system. HIV leads, in many cases, to acquired immunodeficiency syndrome (AIDS), which frequently results in death. Talk to a trusted adult or reliable health-care professional or get public health information from local government agencies or public libraries to learn more about STDs and how to avoid them.

Male reproductive problems

Cancer can develop in the *testicles* and *prostate gland*. Cancer is a disease in which cells multiply wildly, destroying healthy *tissue*. Testicular and prostate cancer can be cured if detected at an early stage. Adolescent boys and men should learn from health-care professionals about testicular self-checking. Adult men should talk to their doctors about prostate care.

Some men produce low numbers of *sperm*, or sperm that are too weak to reach the *fallopian tubes*. Several drugs can help with this problem.

Some men are unable to achieve or maintain an erection. This condition often can be successfully treated in a number of ways, including drugs and dietary changes.

Female reproductive problems

The breasts, *ovaries*, *uterus*, and *cervix* each can develop cancer. Screening, such as cervical smear tests and breast examinations, can detect these cancers at their early stage. Early detection of such cancers can improve the woman's chance for survival. Treatment by surgery, radiation therapy, and chemotherapy often can cure these cancers. Women are advised to check their own breasts regularly and seek medical advice if they notice any changes.

Another female reproductive system disease is endometriosis. In this disease, tissue from the lining of the uterus invades other parts of the abdominal area. It can cause pain, scarring, and infertility. Endometriosis often can be treated with hormones to control the pain, but if it is severe, an operation to remove the tissue may be done.

Ovarian cysts are growths that occur in the ovaries. These cysts can cause pain and bleeding and can interrupt the release of eggs. Ovarian cysts are often removed if their effects become severe.

An ectopic pregnancy arises when a zygote attaches itself to the fallopian tube and begins to grow there instead of in the uterus. An ectopic pregnancy can be very dangerous to the mother, and so the developing baby is usually removed.

FAQ

Q. Can pregnancy cause diabetes?

A. A pregnancy can cause the mother's body to develop a resistance to (action against) insulin that results in a condition called gestational diabetes. Gestational diabetes must be treated to protect the health of the unborn baby and its mother. Gestational diabetes usually disappears after the baby is born.

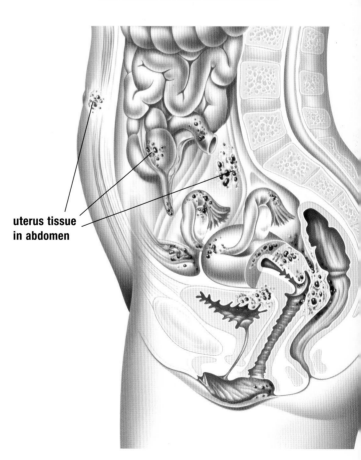

This diagram shows uterus tissue invading other parts of the abdomen. This disease is called endometriosis.

uterus tissue in abdomen

A new life begins

A new life begins when an egg *cell* and a *sperm* cell meet and join together.

Sexual intercourse

Egg and sperm usually meet through an action called sexual intercourse. When a man and a woman are attracted sexually to each other, the man's *penis* becomes erect and the woman's *vagina* becomes lubricated (moist and slippery). The man puts his penis inside the woman's vagina and ejaculates, or releases *semen*.

Fertilization

After the semen has been released into the vagina, thousands of sperm from the semen swim through the *cervix* into the *uterus* and then into the *fallopian tubes*. If a ripe egg cell is in the fallopian tube, some sperm cells cluster around it. Eventually a single sperm cell may manage to get through the jellylike coat that surrounds the egg cell. The egg cell and sperm cell then join together. This is called *fertilization*, or conception.

Sperm clustered around an egg cell. Only one sperm can join with the egg to start a new life.

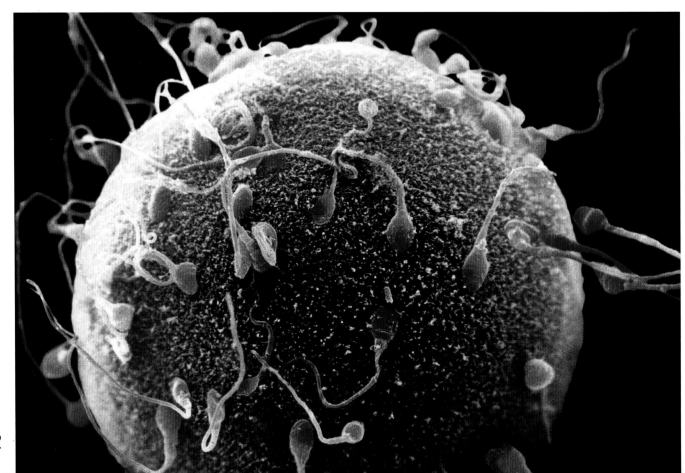

Embryo

The new cell that is made is called a *zygote*. It moves down the fallopian tube toward the uterus. As it travels, it divides to make two new cells. Then each of these cells divides to make two more. Slowly a ball of cells develops, called a morula.

When it reaches the uterus, the morula further develops into a more complex ball of cells called a blastocyst. The blastocyst attaches itself to the uterus lining, or endometrium, where it develops into an *embryo*. The embryo receives nutrients and oxygen from the mother's blood. The cells of the embryo continue to divide, and the embryo eventually grows bigger and bigger. The developing baby is called an embryo through the eighth week of pregnancy.

FAQ

Q. How long does it take a sperm cell to reach the fallopian tubes?

A. Sperm cells can reach the fallopian tubes within as few as five minutes of leaving the penis. Their long, thin tails help them to swim through the cervix and uterus. The tiny hairs on the inside of the fallopian tubes help push the sperm along.

In vitro fertilization

For some couples, sperm and egg do not meet and join, and the couple is said to be infertile. Depending on the cause of their infertility, some couples who want to conceive a child can try a process called in vitro fertilization (IVF). Ripe egg cells taken from the woman and sperm cells taken from the man are mixed together in a laboratory. If fertilization occurs, the resulting zygote can be placed into the woman's uterus, where it can develop and grow into a normal, healthy baby.

Birth control

Sometimes people want to have sexual intercourse but do not want to conceive a baby. Ways to help avoid conceiving a baby are called birth control. The most common type of birth control is called contraception. Several methods can be used for contraception, such as taking a contraceptive drug or using devices to prevent egg and sperm from meeting. Some people disagree about the acceptability of birth control.

During the process of IVF, sperm cells are mixed with egg cells in the laboratory.

During pregnancy

The *embryo* continues to grow and develop during pregnancy. Eventually it will become a *fetus* and then be ready to leave the *uterus* and begin life as a newborn baby.

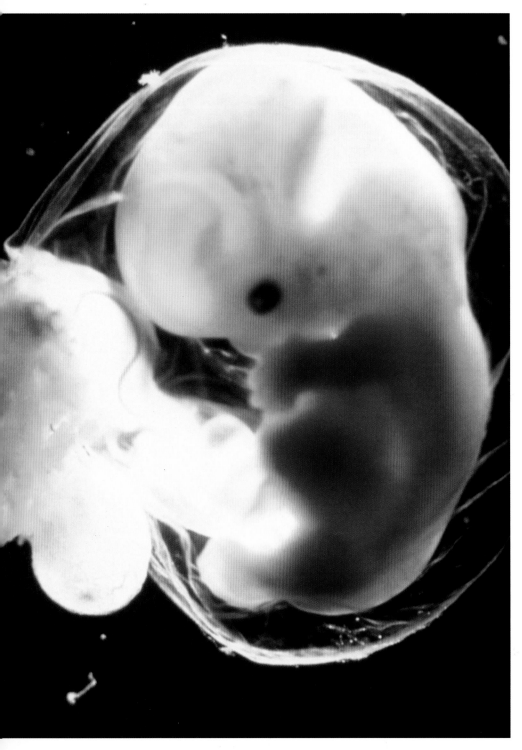

Early development

At first, the embryo is attached directly to the endometrium, the lining of the uterus. Gradually, a network of blood vessels, called the *placenta*, develops between the embryo and the uterus lining. The embryo is attached to the placenta by a cord. This is the umbilical cord, which carries nutrients and oxygen from the mother to the baby. The umbilical cord also carries waste products from the baby to the mother.

The growing embryo is surrounded by a membrane (thin *tissue*) called the *amniotic sac*. This is filled with a liquid, called *amniotic fluid*, which protects and cushions the embryo. The fluid also allows the embryo to move around freely.

A human embryo five or six weeks after fertilization.

Throughout the months before its birth, the baby continues to grow and develop. Its eyes and ears begin to develop in the fourth week of pregnancy; arms and legs begin to appear in the fifth week; fingers and toes develop in the sixth. Starting in the ninth week of pregnancy, the developing baby is called a fetus. After three months, the fetus is about 3 inches (7.6 centimeters) long and weighs about 1 ounce (28 grams). After six months, the fetus is about 14 inches (36 centimeters) long and weighs about 30 ounces (850 grams). After nine months, the fetus is about 20 inches (50 centimeters) long and weighs about 7 pounds (3.2 kilograms).

The mother during pregnancy

The first sign that a woman is pregnant is often when she misses a period. The pregnancy can be confirmed by a pregnancy test. During the next few weeks and months, the woman may experience such symptoms as feeling sick in the mornings, changes in appetite, tiredness, and sore breasts.

As the baby grows, it takes up more and more room inside the woman. This makes her *abdomen* swell, and by the fourth or fifth month the "bump" of the baby is usually visible. The woman's breasts get bigger as they prepare to produce milk for the baby.

Regular medical checks during pregnancy can help to ensure that the mother and unborn baby stay healthy.

FAQ

Q. What should a woman eat when she is pregnant?

A. For the health of herself and her baby, a pregnant woman should eat a healthy, balanced diet before, during, and after her pregnancy. A good diet will ensure that both she and her baby have all the nutrients they need. She should avoid smoking cigarettes and drinking alcohol because these can harm the growing baby. Women who regularly take prescription or over-the-counter medications and who want to become pregnant or learn they are pregnant should talk to a doctor about their continued use of medications.

Birth and the newborn baby

A pregnancy usually lasts 40 weeks, counting from the date of the mother's last period. At the end of this time, the baby is fully developed and ready to be born. Most babies are born headfirst. During the final month of pregnancy, the baby usually turns itself around within the uterus so that it is upside down, with its head above the *cervix*. At the final stages of pregnancy, muscular contractions push the baby out of the uterus and into the outside world.

The process of birth

The process of birth is called labor. The first sign that labor is about to begin is the contracting, or squeezing, of the uterus. Each squeeze is called a contraction. Another early sign is the bursting of the *amniotic sac* and the release of its fluid through the *vagina*.

Medical staff can help and reassure a woman during labor.

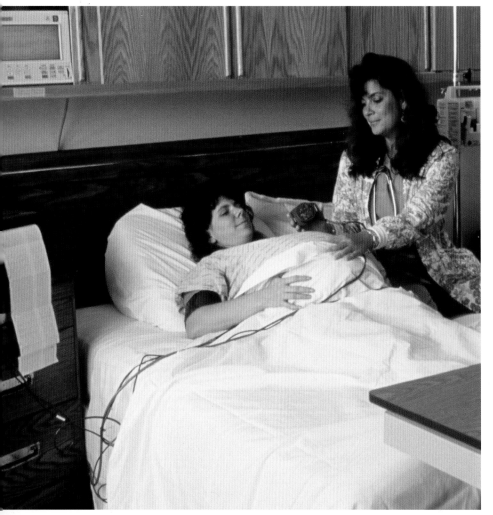

Induced birth

Usually labor begins naturally when the baby is fully developed and ready to be born. But sometimes doctors decide that a baby needs to be born sooner than this, often because the health of the mother or baby is at risk or because the birth process is late in starting. In these cases, doctors can make the birth process begin by giving the mother special drugs. This is called inducing the birth.

The stages of labor

Labor has three stages. At the start of the first stage of labor, contractions are gentle, and long pauses may occur between them. Gradually the contractions become stronger and more frequent. By the end of the first stage of labor, the contractions may occur every two to three minutes. The cervix dilates, or relaxes and widens. Normally the cervix is nearly closed, but it has to widen to about 4 inches (10 centimeters) to let the baby's head pass through.

The second stage of labor begins when the baby's head enters the cervix. The uterus keeps contracting regularly, pushing the baby out of the uterus, through the cervix, and into the vagina. Eventually the baby is forced fully out of the mother's body.

The third stage of labor starts after the baby's delivery. At this stage, the mother and baby are still attached to each other by the *placenta* and umbilical cord.

The newborn baby

As soon as the baby leaves the mother's body, it can begin to breathe on its own. The umbilical cord is cut to separate the baby from the placenta. The stub remains as the navel, or belly button. The baby is usually checked to see that it is healthy, and then the newborn is measured and weighed.

Soon after the baby is born, the placenta breaks away from the uterus and leaves the mother's body through the vagina.

FAQ

Q. What is a cesarean section?

A. Sometimes doctors are concerned about the health of the unborn baby or mother, or the mother may have difficulties delivering the baby through the vagina. In such cases, doctors may perform a cesarean section. A cut is made in the mother's abdomen and uterus, through which the baby is lifted out. The cut is then repaired.

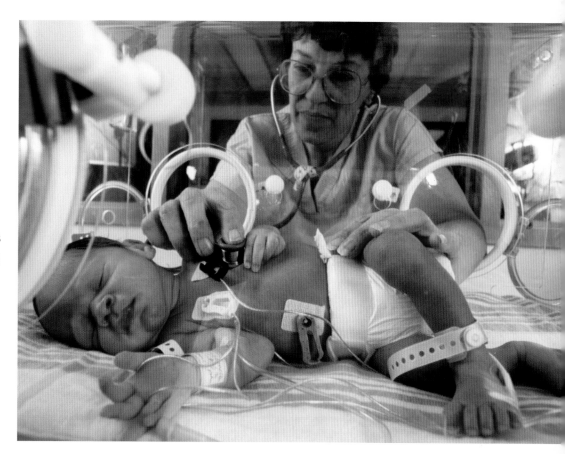

Some newborn babies need to be cared for in an incubator like this one until they are strong enough to go home.

Heredity and genes

People often say that a baby "takes after" a parent or grandparent or that a particular feature "runs in the family." Similarities between family members are caused by *genes*. The passing on of similar characteristics from one generation to the next is called heredity.

Genes

Genes are tiny parts of a certain chemical within *cells* which contain all the information and instructions needed to create and control a living thing. Every cell in the human body has a control center called a nucleus. The nucleus contains 46 threadlike structures called *chromosomes* arranged in 23 pairs. Each chromosome is made up of a sequence of genes, put together in patterns like beads on a necklace. Each gene, or group of genes, carries instructions and information that causes the body to grow, develop, and function.

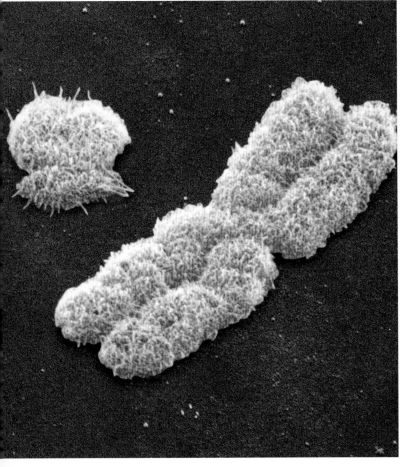

Human sex chromosomes, magnified over 7,000 times. The smaller pair of Y chromosomes is at the top left. The larger pair of X chromosomes is below on the right.

Chromosomes in sex cells

To make an egg cell or a *sperm* cell, an ordinary cell splits in two. Each pair of chromosomes also splits, so that each of the two new cells contains 23 single chromosomes.

When a sperm cell fertilizes an egg cell, the 23 chromosomes from the egg cell join with the 23 chromosomes from the sperm cell, making a new set of 46 chromosomes. This new set of chromosomes contains information from the mother and the father, so the baby that develops will have features from both parents.

Boys and girls

In a set of 23 chromosome pairs, 22 pairs are the same in both boys and girls. One pair is different. These chromosomes are called the

Identical twins like these develop from a single fertilized egg cell.

FAQ

Q. How do twins form?

A. Twins come in two types: identical and non-identical. Identical twins form when the single cell of the *zygote* divides to make two cells. Two identical *embryos* grow and develop into two identical babies. Non-identical, or fraternal, twins form when two eggs are released from the *ovaries* at about the same time and each is separately fertilized. Two different embryos grow and develop into two non-identical babies.

sex chromosomes, and they come in two types: X and Y. Girls have two X chromosomes, and boys have one X and one Y chromosome.

Controlling features

Genes control many features, such as eye color, hair color and texture, and skin color. Each chromosome in a pair carries one version of the same gene. Each gene has two versions: dominant and recessive. Dominant genes overrule recessive genes. For example, the gene for brown eyes (B) is dominant and the gene for blue eyes (b) is recessive. A person with BB genes will have brown eyes. A person with Bb genes also will have brown eyes because the B gene overrules the b gene. To have blue eyes, a person must have two recessive genes, bb.

Inherited diseases and conditions

Genes can carry information and instructions that pass a particular disease or condition from one generation to the next. Hemophilia (a blood disorder) and color blindness are examples of inherited diseases and conditions.

Growth and change

After birth, a baby grows rapidly and begins to learn how to control its body. Growth and development continue throughout childhood and adolescence until adulthood is reached.

Developing skills

A newborn baby is unable to do anything for itself. It cannot turn over or lift its head. It can swallow only liquids so it can eat nothing but milk. It relies on its parents for everything. But it can hear sounds and see light, color, and movement.

A baby grows rapidly, gaining length, weight, and strength. It begins to eat soft food. As the baby's teeth appear, usually beginning during its first year, it is able to eat solid food. By the age of six months, a baby can pick up small objects and pass them from hand to hand. It can sit up without support by about seven months and crawl by about nine months. By the time it is a year old, a baby may be able to stand and walk with support. From the cries of early babyhood, a baby progresses to making burbling noises and then simple, single words by about 12 months.

A baby begins to learn about the world around it through play.

From these early stages, the child learns to control and refine its movements and to improve its coordination and balance. It learns to feed itself and to control its bladder and bowels. Speech and understanding develop, and the child learns to express its own needs and ideas. Throughout childhood, these basic skills develop continually, along with physical growth and development.

Physical growth

Growth does not occur evenly throughout life. The most dramatic period of growth occurs during infancy. By the time most healthy babies are 12 months old, they weigh three times as much as they did when they were born and they are one and a half times as tall. Girls are about half their adult height at 18 months old. Boys are about half their adult height at about two years old.

After the age of four, children grow steadily at about 2 inches (5 centimeters) each year until they reach puberty. Then, under the influence of the sex *hormones*, children experience rapid growth spurts until they reach their full adult height.

FAQ

Q. Does the whole body grow at the same rate?

A. Not all parts of the body grow at the same rate or at the same time. For example, the head grows much less than the legs and trunk. A newborn baby's head is about one-fourth of the length of its body, but an adult's head is only about one-eighth of the length of his or her body.

Height checks during childhood help to monitor growth and development.

Puberty

Puberty is the period during which an individual matures sexually (becomes able to produce offspring, or reproduce). Puberty in human beings usually is the beginning of adolescence. Adolescence is the time during which a child gradually changes physically, mentally, and emotionally to become an adult. Some of the changes can be seen. Others take place inside the body, and so they cannot be seen. In healthy individuals, puberty and adolescence usually begin between the ages of 10 and 12. Girls usually reach puberty earlier than boys. And the rate of sexual development of boys and girls generally differs.

Some of the changes that take place at puberty can be seen.

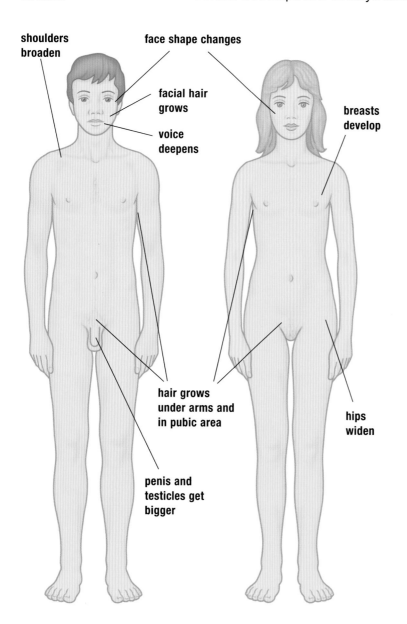

shoulders broaden

face shape changes

facial hair grows

voice deepens

breasts develop

hair grows under arms and in pubic area

hips widen

penis and testicles get bigger

The start of puberty

Puberty is triggered when sex *hormones* are released by the brain and sex organs. In both boys and girls, the *hypothalamus* releases a hormone. This makes the *pituitary gland* release two hormones, follicle-stimulating hormone (FSH) and luteinizing hormone (LH). FSH and LH stimulate the sex organs to produce sex hormones. In boys, the *testicles* release testosterone. In girls, the *ovaries* release estrogens and progesterone. Testosterone, estrogens, and progesterone cause the changes that take place during puberty.

Changes in boys and girls

During puberty the following changes take place in both boys and girls:

• sudden growth spurts
• lengthening of the face
• appearance of body hair
• increased oiliness of skin
• possible increase of body odor.

Changes in boys

The following changes take place only in boys:

- deepening of the voice
- widening of the shoulders
- increase in size of *penis* and testicles
- beginning of *sperm* production.

Changes in girls

The following changes take place only in girls:

- widening of the hips
- development of the breasts
- development of the ovaries
- beginning of ripening of egg *cells*
- beginning of *menstruation*.

Ovary development and egg ripening take place inside the body, and so they cannot be seen, but the onset of menstruation shows that these changes are taking place.

FAQ

Q. What is the "history" of adolescence?

A. Recognition of the period of human development today known as adolescence grew out of changes in human society of the late 1800's and early 1900's. Starting then, fewer young people farmed or did other work in the family, so they were set apart and given special preparation for adulthood. That period of preparation became identified as adolescence.

During puberty, we change from being a child to an adult.

Adolescence

Along with the physical changes that people experience during puberty and adolescence, they experience emotional and intellectual changes.

Increasing independence

As they mature, or get older, many teenagers feel they should have more freedom and independence. They often want to make their own decisions about things that affect them. Many parents feel that their adolescent sons and daughters are too young to be given these freedoms.

New ways of thinking

As people mature, they begin to think in a more abstract way. "Abstract" means having to do with ideas or concepts rather than particular things. Maturing people may take an interest in such topics as relationships, politics, religion, and ethics (ideas about right and wrong). They begin to question more and be able to think about different opinions. During childhood, a simple decision between right and wrong is often easy to make. Life can seem more complicated for a teenager, however. Teenagers may have to make decisions about staying in school, smoking cigarettes, drinking alcohol,

During adolescence, many people develop new relationships and friends.

taking drugs, or having sexual relationships. Making these decisions can be even harder when friends and classmates encourage one thing or another.

Changing relationships

Adolescents may find that their attitudes about family and friends can change, too. Childhood friendships may be replaced by new friendships that reflect a teenager's new ways of thinking. Relationships within the family may change if teenagers start to spend more time alone or with people outside their family and less time with parents, brothers, and sisters. Teenagers sometimes feel sexually attracted to another person. They often start to make special times, or dates, with other people as a way to explore such feelings.

FAQ

Q. Why do we have sexual dreams and fantasies?

A. As the body changes during puberty and adolescence, the brain makes some adjustments too. These adjustments often include dreaming and fantasizing about emotional and sexual relationships. Many boys have "wet dreams," when *semen* is released while they sleep. People may fantasize about relationships with others their own age whom they know or with sports and entertainment celebrities. Such dreaming and fantasizing are ways the body and mind help prepare us for actual relationships.

Adolescents sometimes find it difficult to understand their parents' point of view.

Glossary

abdomen The segment of the human body between the chest and pelvis (bony structure below the abdomen).

adrenal gland One of two glands that produce epinephrine and corticosteroids.

amniotic fluid A liquid that surrounds the embryo during pregnancy.

amniotic sac A baglike membrane inside the uterus that holds amniotic fluid and the developing baby.

cell One of the tiny units from which all living things are made.

cervix The opening between the uterus and the vagina.

chromosome The part of the cell that carries genetic information.

embryo An unborn baby in the early stage of development.

epididymis (plural: epididymides) A coiled tube in which sperm mature.

exocrine gland A gland that produces liquids such as saliva and sweat.

fallopian tube A tube that links an ovary with the uterus.

fertilization The union of sperm and egg cells.

fetus An unborn baby after eight weeks of development.

gene One of the small chemical units that make up a chromosome.

gland A structure in the body that produces hormones or other chemicals.

hormone A chemical produced by a gland that travels in the blood and affects another part or a function of the body.

hypothalamus A gland that controls the pituitary gland and parts of the nervous system.

menstruation The loss of blood and the uterus lining each month in women of childbearing age who are not pregnant.

ovary One of two female reproductive organs that produce and store eggs.

ovulation The release of an egg from an ovary.

pancreas A structure in the body that produces some digestive juices and some hormones.

parathyroid gland One of four glands that produce parathyroid hormone (PTH).

penis The male reproductive organ through which urine and semen are released.

pineal gland A gland that produces melatonin.

pituitary gland A gland that produces hormones that affect many parts of the body, including other endocrine glands.

placenta A body structure that links embryo and mother.

prostate gland A gland involved in the production of seminal fluid.

protein Large, complex chemicals that form the building blocks of living things.

scrotum The external pouch of skin and muscle at the base of the abdomen that holds the testicles.

semen A mixture of sperm and seminal fluid.

sperm A cell from a male that can fertilize an egg.

testicle One of the two male organs that produce sperm.

thymus gland A gland that produces thymosin and is also involved in the body's defense system.

thyroid gland A gland that produces hormones, including thyroxine and calcitonin.

tissue A part of the body made from cells that are all similar. Muscles are one kind of tissue, and skin is another.

urethra A tube through which semen and urine leave the male body and through which urine leaves the female body.

urine Waste in liquid form produced by the kidneys and stored in the bladder before being eliminated from the body.

uterus The hollow muscular organ in which an unborn baby develops during pregnancy.

vagina The organ that links female reproductive organs to the outside of the body.

vas deferens (plural: vas deferentia) A tube through which sperm travel from testicle to urethra.

vulva The external female sexual organs.

zygote A fertilized egg.

Additional resources

Books

Miller, Michaela. *Exploring the Human Body: Reproduction and Growth*. San Diego, CA: KidHaven Press, 2005.

Parker, Steve. *Our Bodies: Reproduction*. Chicago: Raintree, 2004.

Silverstein, Robert. *Human Body Systems: Reproductive System.* New York: Twenty-First Century Books, 1997.

Walker, Pam and Elaine Wood. *Understanding the Human Body: The Reproductive System.* San Diego, CA: Lucent Books, 2003.

Web sites

http://www.kidshealth.org/
An entertaining guide to the human body, including sections on the endocrine and reproductive systems.

http://www.bbc.co.uk/science/humanbody/
BBC Human Body and Mind, an interactive Web site with information on puberty.

http://arbl.cvmbs.colostate.edu/hbooks/pathphys/endocrine/
An in-depth guide to the endocrine system.

Index

Page numbers in **bold** refer to illustrations.